IT'S JUST AGING

A STORY ABOUT GROWING UP!

Written By
Eliah Takushi, Carly Tan, & Colby Takeda

Illustrated by
Jamie Meckel Tablason

Scripta

Honolulu, Hawai'i

My name is Lily, and this is my Tūtū.

Tūtū knows a lot of things because she has lived a long time. She teaches me how to make plumeria lei, play the ʻukulele, and catch waves with my surfboard.

Today, she will teach me how to make her famous banana bread, which she makes in a rice cooker—it's so ʻono! We grab the shopping list and head to the market.

I look in the mirror and see Tūtū driving. I have Tūtū's nose; it's cute and button-sized. I have Tūtū's eyes; they're big and brown.

My hair is black, but Tūtū's hair is gray. "Tūtū, why is your hair gray?"

"*It's just aging*," Tūtū says.

"Aging is when you get older and over time, people may start to look a little different. In Hawai'i, we call older people kūpuna, because they are wise and have lots of experience."

Tūtū says that we all go through aging and that it's normal. She says that even bananas age, and when they do, they're perfect for making banana bread.

Tūtū asks me to grab the sugar, so I run down the aisle and see a kupuna with gray hair, just like my Tūtū. "Excuse me, could you hand me a bag of sugar?" I kindly ask. He doesn't respond.

I ask him again, "Excuse me, could you please hand me a bag of sugar?" He still doesn't respond.

Tūtū comes to the rescue and taps the kupuna on the shoulder. She asks in a loud voice, **"Excuse me, could you please pass me a bag of sugar?"**

"I'm so sorry. I forgot my hearing aid at home and can't hear a thing without it," says the kupuna as he hands Tūtū the sugar. **"Mahalo,"** Tūtū replies.

Tūtū says that hearing loss is normal, but that hearing aids can help. She says it's best to speak loud and clear when talking to kūpuna and not to become frustrated if they have difficulties hearing you—*it's just aging*.

When we get home, I run outside and see my grandpa watering his beautiful orchids. I call my grandpa Papa. Papa teaches me about the different plants and fruit trees in his garden, and I especially love his apple bananas because they are extra sweet and slightly tart.

"Aloha, Papa! Tūtū and I are making banana bread and need five ripe apple bananas."

"No problem, Lily," Papa responds.

Papa uses his cane to pull down a bunch of apple bananas. He picks off five ripe apple bananas and hands them to me to bring inside.

"Why does Papa have a cane?" I ask Tūtū.

"When people get older, their muscles weaken and they may need a cane, a walker, or even a wheelchair to help them get around," Tūtū replies.

Papa brings his cane everywhere. I have always wondered why he walks with that stick, but now I know that canes aren't weird—*it's just aging.*

I mash up the apple bananas, mix them with the other ingredients, and pour the batter into the rice cooker. I start the rice cooker and wait with excitement.

"Beep! Beep!" goes the rice cooker. "Tūtū, it's done!" I can already smell the bread and can't wait to try it.

Tūtū cuts me a slice of the warm banana bread, and I take a bite.

It's sweet, fluffy, and so yummy!

I wrap up a few slices and walk down the street to Auntie Nani's house.

"Aloha, Auntie Nani! Tūtū just taught me how to make her famous banana bread, and I brought you some to try."

"Mahalo, Lily! You're growing up so fast, and now you can make your Tūtū's banana bread!" said Auntie Nani.

"Yup! *It's just aging…* and I love it!"

Tūtū's Banana Bread

Ingredients:
1 cup flour
2 tsp baking powder
1/2 tsp baking soda
1/2 tsp salt
1/2 cup white sugar
5 ripe apple bananas
1/3 cup cooking oil
1/8 cup milk
1 egg

In a mixing bowl, combine all ingredients and mix until smooth. Butter you rice cooker pan and pour in the batter. Cook in the rice cooker until done (this may take multiple cycles).

Optional:
Add cinnamon, agave, or other fruit to the batter, or top with apricot jam or roasted pistachios.

The Plaza Assisted Living currently serves Hawaii's seniors from five assisted living communities throughout Oʻahu and strives to foster independence in their residents, support their loved ones, and empower their employees to make a difference. The Plaza Assisted Living is proud to support the production of this book in hopes that it helps to develop strong intergenerational relationships and reduce negative perceptions about kūpuna.

Through our **Pages With All Ages** program, residents at The Plaza Assisted Living will share pieces of literature–such as *It's Just Aging*–with keiki and have meaningful conversations about getting older. Please join us in strengthening the connection between our keiki and kūpuna and celebrating all that these two generations have to offer.

Learn more about
Pages With All Ages at
www.plazaassistedliving.com

THE **PLAZA**
—Assisted Living—

For Kyla
You will always be our little princess

Eliah Takushi & Carly Tan are both proud members of the ʻIolani School class of 2017 and were inspired to create a children's story while in the One Mile Project class. Eliah is passionate about anime, singing off-key in the shower, and spending quality time with both of her grandmothers. Carly enjoys listening to and performing music, babysitting her little brother, and dancing like no one's watching. They both hope that through this fun story, children will see kūpuna in a different light and will appreciate everything that older adults have to offer. Of course, you can't go wrong with some freshly baked banana bread either!

Colby Takeda is an administrator with The Plaza Assisted Living and loves being around Hawaiʻi's intelligent, talented, and caring kūpuna on a daily basis. At the same time, he finds great joy in working with youth and is a high school track & field coach and advisor for Bridge Club Hawaiʻi, a youth organization that he established in 2009. Colby is a graduate of ʻIolani School and received his B.A. from Willamette University in Salem, Oregon.

Jamie Meckel Tablason loves illustrating picture books for children as much as she loves the islands. She grew up and lives in Southern California with her husband and two dogs. She earned her B.F.A. and M.F.A. in illustration from CSU Long Beach.

ISBN-13: 978-0-9844458-6-8
Library of Congress Control Number: 2015909751

Text by Eliah Takushi, Carly Tan, and Colby Takeda
Illustrations by Jamie Meckel Tablason

First Printing, November 2015

The Plaza Assisted Living
900 Fort Street Mall, Suite 1722
Honolulu, Hawaiʻi 96813
Ph: 808-955-0800

Produced by:
Mutual Publishing, LLC
1215 Center Street, Suite 210
Honolulu, Hawaiʻi 96816
Ph: (808) 732-1709 / Fax: (808) 734-4094
email: info@mutualpublishing.com
www.mutualpublishing.com

Printed in China

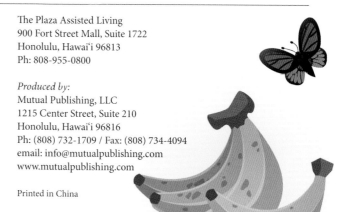